T0015411

THE AUTHORITY OF THE COURT
AND THE PERIL OF POLITICS

The Scalia Lecture, 2021

THE

Authority *of* *the* Court *and the* Peril *of* Politics

STEPHEN BREYER

Harvard University Press

CAMBRIDGE, MASSACHUSETTS | LONDON, ENGLAND

2021

Image credits:

Fig. 1 is reformatted from Hannah Hartig, "Before Ginsburg's
Death, a Majority of Americans Viewed the Supreme Court as
'Middle of the Road,'" Pew Research Center, September 25,
2020, https://www.pewresearch.org/fact-tank/2020/09/25
/before-ginsburgs-death-a-majority-of-americans-viewed-the
-supreme-court-as-middle-of-the-road.

Fig. 2 is reformatted from "Public Trust in Government:
1958–2019," Pew Research Center, April 11, 2019,
http://www.pewresearch.org/politics/2019/04/11
/public-trust-in-government-1958-2019.

Library of Congress Cataloging-in-Publication Data

Names: Breyer, Stephen G., 1938– author.
Title: The authority of the Court and the peril of
politics / Stephen Breyer.
Identifiers: LCCN 2021017885 |
ISBN 9780674269361 (cloth)
Subjects: LCSH: United States. Supreme Court. |
Rule of law—United States. | Political questions and
judicial power—United States.
Classification: LCC KF8742 .B7279 2021 |
DDC 347.73 / 262—dc23
LC record available at https://lccn.loc.gov/2021017885

Dedicated to all my grandchildren,
Clara, Ancel, Eli, Samuel, Angela, and Stevie

CONTENTS

Some years ago the chief justice of the Supreme Court of Ghana came to visit our Court. She wanted to learn how the US Supreme Court had advanced and protected civil rights in America. She seemed particularly interested in this question: Why does the American public do what the Supreme Court says? Implicitly she also wanted to know why, or how, the Court could act as a check upon other parts of government, even presidents, where there is serious disagreement among the branches. These are indeed important questions.

Put abstractly, the Court's power, like that of any tribunal, must depend upon the public's willingness to respect its decisions—even those with which they disagree, and even when they believe a decision seriously mistaken. Such respect matters most when a decision of the Court strongly conflicts with the expressed views of those in other branches, most notably the president. After all, the Court is without its own means to enforce its views directly, being reliant for this on the executive.

This essay will expand on the importance of public acceptance in safeguarding the role of the judiciary. The first part, to provide context, will set forth several examples illustrating the increase in the public's acceptance of the Court's decisions, and with it an increase in the Court's authority. The second and third parts will discuss more directly the Court's related power to act as a check upon the rest of the government. I shall illustrate the kinds of checks that I have in mind. I shall also illustrate how the Court's power to check has grown over time, with the public's acceptance of its authority. And I shall describe certain related, potential difficulties that may arise in the future. I will then propose a few steps the Court and public could take to help overcome these problems.

AUTHOR'S NOTE

I had originally prepared the following as remarks for a presentation in France. The topic was to be "The Supreme Court: Power and Counter-Power." Because of the difficulties of traveling to France, I decided to use these remarks as the basis for the 2021 Scalia Lecture at Harvard Law School and then to publish the resulting lecture in edited form. I believe this essay, reflecting in part my own experience, is relevant to recent disagreements over the nature and future of the Court. There are different, often competing, views about the Court's proper role. And in recent months, the topic has often been discussed more intensely. Here I seek, in simplified form and through examples, to show how I believe the

Court obtained power, the nature of that power, and some of the challenges now facing the Court. I also make several general suggestions about what the Court and the country might do to minimize the risks associated with those challenges. They are general suggestions; they do not purport to provide specific solutions to the problems that the judiciary faces.

June 2021

I

The Court's Power: In General

Why will people follow the suggestions, thoughts, even the orders of others? Long ago Cicero described an answer to this central question about the nature of power. He thought there were three possible ways to assure the obedience of those who live in a state: 1) the fear of punishment; 2) the hope of rewards or particular benefits; and 3) the perception that the state is a just one. This last way, justice, was to convince people that those who govern *deserve* obedience. Whether Cicero's view does or does not apply in general to government, it certainly applies to the US Supreme Court. The Court's ability to punish or to provide rewards or benefits is limited. Its ability to act justly, at least in my view, does play a major role in obtaining the public's respect and consequent obedience. The Court's history illustrates how that is so. A few examples will help support this point of view.

THE AUTHORITY OF THE COURT

In considering those examples, it is important to keep in mind how the law provides the Court with legal power. That power has its principal source in the US Constitution as well as in the views of those who wrote it. The Constitution is a brief document. It has seven articles and twenty-seven amendments. It creates a representative federal democracy, with a separation of governmental powers both horizontal (legislative, executive, judicial) and vertical (state and federal); equality of individuals before the law; protection of fundamental rights; and a guarantee of the rule of law. The Constitution's framers had every right to admire their creation. But, as Alexander Hamilton points out in *Federalist* 78, one branch of government must have authority to assure that the other branches act within the limits set by the Constitution. Otherwise the document will have little effect; the framers might as well have hung it on the walls of a museum.

Which branch will have the authority to determine what limits the Constitution sets forth and when a branch has exceeded them? The executive branch, namely, the president? Is there not a risk that the president would simply decide that whatever action he or she takes is consistent with the Constitution? What about Congress? Its members are popularly elected; they likely understand popularity. What would happen when, say, those entitled to constitutional protections are not popular? The Constitution, indeed law in general, applies to those who are not popular just as it applies to those who are popular. Can Congress be trusted to protect the unpopular?

The third branch, the judiciary, remains. Very good, Hamilton might have thought. Judges understand law. They are unlikely to become too powerful, for they lack the power of purse and of sword. Hence the judicial branch and the Supreme Court in particular should have the last word. The majority of the other framers agreed with Hamilton. But the acceptance of this view was not inevitable, nor was it to come without a long struggle. Unlike Hamilton, Thomas Jefferson was unwilling to give judges the ultimate power to resolve constitutional and statutory conflicts, particularly at a time of heightened partisanship, when the judiciary was perceived as favoring Jefferson's political opponents, the Federalists. Indeed, Jefferson once wrote, "Each of the three departments has equally the right to decide for itself what is its duty under the constitution, *without any regard to what the others may have decided for themselves under a similar question.*"[1] As far as Jefferson was concerned, the less powerful the Supreme Court, the better.

It was Hamilton's view that Chief Justice John Marshall and the Supreme Court adopted in the famous 1803 case *Marbury v. Madison.*[2] The case arose at the time of the "midnight judges." John Adams, a Federalist, had just lost the presidential election to Jefferson, a Democratic-Republican (now the Democratic Party). Adams quickly nominated

[1] *The Works of Thomas Jefferson,* ed. Paul Leicester Ford, vol. 12 (New York: G. P. Putnam, 1905), 139 (emphasis added).

[2] 5 US 137 (1803).

several judges; the Senate, within a few days, confirmed them. All that remained was for Adams to deliver their commissions in time—that is, before his term as president expired. Adams failed to deliver William Marbury's commission on time. Did that mean that Marbury was not a judge?

Marbury brought a case in the Supreme Court. He asked the Court to order the new president, Jefferson, to deliver his commission. Marbury seemed likely correct in stating that the law required Jefferson to do so. Still, the request placed the Court on the horns of a dilemma. On the one hand, suppose the Court held that the law did *not* entitle Marbury to his commission. That decision would suggest to many that the Court was a weak institution, that it had departed from what the law seemed to require for fear that the president would simply ignore its decision. This would have been to suggest that courts, and perhaps the law itself, could not stand in the way of a determined president. On the other hand, if the Court held that the law *did* entitle Marbury to his commission, Jefferson (who saw the judges as enemies and who thought his own conduct exemplary) might still ignore the Court. In that case, the resulting message would be the same: the president was free to choose whether to accept the Court's decisions.

Chief Justice Marshall, writing for a unanimous court, found a brilliant way out. The Court first held that the law did, as many thought, entitle Marbury to his commission. The Court thereby asserted the right to decide whether an action (or inaction) on the part of the president violated the law—a right Hamilton believed was properly the Court's. But the Court also held that Jefferson, not Marbury, must prevail because the statutory provision that granted the Supreme Court the power to hear Marbury's case was unconstitutional. In finding a law of Congress unconstitutional, Chief Justice Marshall again adopted Hamilton's views. Marshall strengthened the norm of judicial review, exercising for the first time the Court's authority to strike down a law as unconstitutional, and he did so in a way strategically designed to avoid the risk that the president would ignore what the Court ordered. The chief justice thereby circumvented the threat that the Court's role in American society would be undermined.

Marbury v. Madison, however, is only the beginning of the story. It does not show that a president will do what the Court says. In Shakespeare's *Henry IV, Part I,* Owen Glendower, who is Welsh and a mystic, boasts to the rebel Hotspur, "I can call spirits from the vasty deep." "Why, so can I," Hotspur replies, "or so can any man. But will they come, when you do call for them?" I have said that the Constitution's words and the framers' intent were a source of the Supreme Court's power only *in part,* because neither Hamilton nor any other framer has a good answer to Hotspur's critical question.

EXAMPLE: A POWERLESS OPINION

Indeed, on one of the first occasions when the Court and the president found themselves in conflict on an important matter, the president prevailed. Early in the history of the republic, a tribe of Indians, the

Cherokee, lived in northern Georgia on land that treaties guaranteed them. In 1829 gold was found on that land. The Georgians wanted the gold, and the state took control of the Cherokees' land. The Cherokees and their supporters found an excellent lawyer, William Wirt, to vindicate their treaty rights. Wirt filed complaints in court, and eventually the issue of territorial control found its way to the Supreme Court.

The Court found in *Worcester v. Georgia* that the Cherokees had the legal right to control their territory and that Georgia lacked legal authority to do so.[3] The state of Georgia, however, simply ignored the Court's decision. What did Andrew Jackson, president of the United States, do? Nothing. He is supposed to have said, "John Marshall has made his decision; now let him enforce it." Jackson (and his successor) then sent federal troops to Georgia but not to enforce the Court's judgment.[4] Rather, he sent

[3] 31 US 515 (1832).

[4] Leonard Baker, *John Marshall: A Life in Law* (New York: Macmillan, 1974), 745.

them to remove the Cherokees, forcing many of them to travel on the Trail of Tears to Oklahoma, where their descendants live to this day.

Would presidents respect decisions of the Supreme Court when they hold strongly contrary views? The case was not a happy omen.

Supreme Court justices would long remain uncertain whether the Court could sustain a judgment that other branches or the public strongly opposed. In 1903 Justice Oliver Wendell Holmes Jr. summed up the problem in a decision that effectively refused to enforce the Fifteenth Amendment's guarantee that former slaves could vote. How could Holmes have done this? He wrote that the Court has "little practical power to deal with the people of the state in a body." He added, it was said that "the great mass of the white population intends to keep the blacks from voting." If that was so, a Court decision ordering the contrary would be "an empty form."[5] The power to redress that evil must lie in the hands of the legislature and the executive, Holmes concluded.

[5] Giles v. Harris, 189 US 475, 488 (1903).

THE AUTHORITY OF THE COURT

Where then lies the power of the Supreme Court?

The 1930s saw a political-judicial struggle that focused upon, but did not answer, that question. In the early 1930s, the country fell into economic depression, causing enormous suffering across the nation. A new president, Franklin Roosevelt, presented a New Deal designed to help, but the Court struck down much of the attendant legislation as unconstitutional. At the time three of the justices—Louis Brandeis, Harlan Stone, and Benjamin Cardozo, referred to as the Three Musketeers—consistently supported President Roosevelt's legislative agenda. The so-called Four Horsemen—Justices Willis Van Devanter, James McReynolds, George Sutherland, and Pierce Butler—could be counted on to oppose New Deal legislation. The two remaining justices, Chief Justice Charles Evans Hughes and Justice Owen Roberts, sided with the opponents of Roosevelt's New Deal legislation in some, but not all, key cases. Between 1933 and 1936, the Court overturned federal legislation at ten times the rate it had in previous years.

Many believed that the Court had left Roosevelt's initial New Deal recovery plan in tatters. Secretary of the Interior Harold Ickes described the resulting dilemma in these terms: reform the Court or submit to "judicial tyranny."[6]

In November 1936 Roosevelt was reelected in a landslide, the largest in the nation's history. He won 61 percent of the popular vote and nearly the entire electoral college. Viewing this popularity as a mandate to continue to build upon his achievements of the prior term, which were substantial despite those that were overturned, Roosevelt planned an ambitious legislative agenda. But what was he to do about the Supreme Court?

In February 1937 Roosevelt devised a plan to "reorganize" the federal judiciary. The plan, the Judicial Procedures Reform Act, included a provision authorizing the president to appoint a new justice for

[6] Jeff Shesol, *Supreme Power: Franklin Roosevelt vs. the Supreme Court* (New York: W. W. Norton, 2010), 3.

each sitting justice over the age of seventy years and six months. Given the age of the then-sitting justices, the proposal would have assured Roosevelt the immediate authority to appoint six new justices to the Court. Roosevelt publicly justified this legislative initiative as necessary to meet the Court's burgeoning workload. He pointed to the large number of civil cases denied through the certiorari process and to the ages of the sitting justices. But few doubted the true objective of the plan: packing the court with judges who would be less likely to void New Deal policies.

From the start there was vigorous opposition to the plan, even in a strongly pro-Roosevelt Congress. Many legislators feared changes to the structure of the nation's government, particularly changes that would weaken the checks and balances the framers had established. And these legislators thought that a majority of the public felt the same way they did. But Roosevelt continued to press for enactment of the Judicial Procedures Reform Act.

Then, later in 1937, the Court handed Roosevelt and his supporters a key victory. By a vote of five to four, the Court took the view that Congress had the power to regulate labor relations. Justice Roberts was considered to have provided the key swing vote. The case, *National Labor Relations Board v. Jones & Laughlin Steel Corporation,* was soon seen as representing a major change in the Court's general jurisprudential approach.[7] Previously the Court had tended to find economic-reform legislation an unconstitutional curtailment of liberty and freedom of contract. This was the defining feature of the so-called Lochner era, named for *Lochner v. New York,* the 1905 case in which the Court struck down a New York state law limiting the workday of bakery employees to ten hours. Now, after the *NLRB* case, the Court would interpret the Constitution as granting to government far more leeway to enact economic and social legislation.[8] This jurisprudential shift, the effective end of the Court's laissez-faire Lochner era, coupled with Justice Van Devanter's retirement

[7] 301 US 1 (1937). See also West Coast Hotel v. Parrish, 300 US 379 (1937).

[8] 198 US 45 (1905).

at the end of the 1937 term, essentially put an end to Roosevelt's judicial reform bill. It no longer seemed necessary to its supporters.

Scholars disagree as to just what caused the justices to change course.[9] Was it a "switch in time" that "saved nine"—a move calculated to avoid Roosevelt's court-packing plan? Or was it simply the coming to fruition of a long-standing jurisprudential debate among the justices—a debate that originated well before the appearance of the court-packing threat and continued well after? Perhaps Justice Roberts knew. Others do not.

However much by design, the Court avoided a politically motivated institutional change. Roosevelt's reform bill failed. The Court remained a nine-justice panel. But at the same time, the Court's driving jurisprudential views changed. So who won? Scholars

[9] See Barry Cushman, "Rethinking the New Deal Court," *Virginia Law Review* 80, no. 1 (1994): 201–261, 201, 207.

can argue about how much the court-packing episode tells us about the Court's power. I shall not.

The court-packing story, however, is relevant here for another reason. Proposals have been recently made to increase the number of Supreme Court justices. Others will, no doubt, discuss the related political arguments. For example, will what goes around come around? That is, will future Congresses and presidents engage in ever more court packing in order to shift the Court's balance in their own favor? Are the nomination and confirmation processes working well? Do appointments too closely reflect partisan political divisions? Has the Court itself become politically partisan? This essay will not delve into such issues. Instead, my goal is to ensure that those who debate these proposals also consider an important institutional point, namely how a proposed change could affect the rule of law itself.

To discuss this institutional question, it is necessary to focus upon more than the rights and wrongs of individual cases, however important. When justices dissent, we typically think the majority is wrong, sometimes very wrong. But discussion of major changes should take account of certain background considerations, such as the trust that the Court has gradually built, the long period of time needed to build that trust, and the importance of that trust in a diverse nation that values, indeed depends upon, a rule of law.

In writing this, my aim is to supply background, particularly for those who are not judges or lawyers, that will facilitate a discussion sensitive to historical context and the relationship among public trust, the Court's authority, and the rule of law. Indeed, I aim to make those whose reflexive instincts may favor significant structural (or other important) changes, such as forms of court packing, think long and hard before embodying those changes in law.

EXAMPLE: THE GROWTH OF THE COURT'S POWER

Let us now jump to 1954. In that year the Court held that law-based racial segregation, practiced widely in the South, violated the Fourteenth Amendment's guarantee that the law must provide every "person . . . equal protection." The Court's decision, in *Brown v. Board of Education,* sounds perfectly straightforward.[10] But what actually happened next, in 1955? Virtually nothing. And in 1956? Almost nothing again. Congress did nothing. The president did little. And the South complied only minimally with the Court's ruling.

In 1957, however, a federal trial court judge in Little Rock, Arkansas, ordered the state to enroll nine black students at Central High, an all-white school. On the first day of classes in September, a large and hostile crowd surrounded Central High. The governor, Orval Faubus, announced his opposition to integration and sent state police to prevent the nine black students from entering the school. A standoff ensued, lasting several days. Journalists from around the world came to cover the event. The

[10] 347 US 483 (1954).

question on everyone's mind: What would the president of the United States do?

James Byrnes, then governor of South Carolina, as well as a former Supreme Court justice, wartime economic administrator, and a "moderate" on race, advised President Eisenhower to do nothing. He told the president that if he sent troops to Arkansas, there could well be violence. The federal government might have to occupy the South, and Eisenhower would have a second Reconstruction on his hands. At best, the South would close all its schools. But Herbert Brownell, the US attorney general, took the opposite position. He told the president he must send troops, if for no other reason than to protect the rule of law. In the end, the president decided to send a thousand parachutists from the 101st Airborne Division. At the time, nearly all Americans recognized that division as heroes of the American invasion of Normandy and the Battle of the Bulge. The parachutists took the nine brave black students by the hand and walked them into the formerly white school. So the Court won this confrontation, did it not? It did, but it won *with* the cooperation of the president of the United States.

Moreover, the story does not end there. The troops could not stay at the school forever. After several months they withdrew, and the local authorities then tried to resegregate Central High. In the resulting case of *Cooper v. Aaron,* the Supreme Court rejected their attempt.[11] It ordered immediate integration. But local authorities would not comply. In fact, they went so far as to close the school. That year, no student at Central High, white or black, received an education.

The situation could not last. This was the time of Martin Luther King Jr., of bus boycotts, of freedom riders. The nation had awakened to the injustice of racial segregation. And by the time of King's assassination in April of 1968, racial segregation imposed by law ended in the South of the United States.

I once asked Vernon Jordan, the great civil rights leader (who recently died), whether the Court had actually played a major role in ending segregation.

[11] 358 US 1 (1958).

After all, even absent the Court would there not have been enormous pressure to end that system—pressure from civil rights leaders, from the rest of the country, indeed from the entire world? He answered that of course the Court had been critically important. Congress, after all, had done nothing before *Brown*. At the very least, the Court had provided a catalyst. In concert with other actors, it had succeeded in toppling a significant pillar if not of racism then at least of racism's legal architecture. The Court had not done it alone but nevertheless had played an essential role in ending legal segregation. Together with the president, civil rights leaders, and a great many ordinary citizens, the Court had won a major victory for constitutional law, for equality, and above all for justice itself. And in turn, justice itself—the justice of the Court's integration decisions—helped to promote respect for the Court and increased its authority. I cannot prove this assertion. But I fervently believe it.

EXAMPLE: AN ATMOSPHERE OF RESPECT

A further example to which I would call attention is the Court's decision in *Bush v. Gore.*[12] It is debatable whether that decision actually determined who would be president of the United States. But many thought that it did. At the least, the decision was a highly important one, potentially affecting vast numbers of Americans. The Court divided five to four. I did not agree with the majority. In fact, I wrote a dissenting opinion.

At the time of *Bush v. Gore,* Harry Reid was Senate minority whip, and, as a Democrat, not likely to have welcomed the decision. But he would later say that its most remarkable feature may have been one on which few had then remarked: despite the huge stakes involved, despite the belief of half the country that the Court was misguided, Americans accepted the majority's holding without violent protest, without the throwing of stones in the streets.

[12] 531 US 98 (2000).

And the losing candidate, Al Gore, told his supporters, "Don't trash the Supreme Court."[13]

These facts suggest that acceptance of the Court's decisions, respect for those decisions even when one considers them wrong, had become virtually habitual. Americans still mostly find this a normal attitude to take. Indeed, this attitude is so normal that hardly anyone notices it. As the air around us, also unnoticed, allows us to breathe, so too this habit allows the rule of law to persist and flourish.

One might argue that Americans have too readily accepted Court decisions that are "wrong." What about decisions finding a constitutional right to keep handguns? Or to have abortions? Or decisions finding in the First Amendment a prohibition against certain political campaign contributions? Or any number of things a great many Americans consider objection-

[13] Adam Nagourney, "Everyone Has a Game Plan until You Punch Them in the Mouth," *New York Times Magazine,* March 2, 2014.

able? The list does go on, its length and content depending upon who is asked to write it.

Whether particular decisions are right or wrong, however, is not the issue here. Nor is the validity of different approaches to legal or constitutional interpretation. Rather, I am discussing the general tendency of the public to respect and to follow judicial decisions, a habit developed over the course of American history. Were it not the case, courts that the public tended to ignore would not see their interpretations of law applied generally, as they are in our system. Parties who disagree with a particular decision, focusing upon its particular stakes, might be unperturbed by such a situation. But what, then, would have happened to all those Americans who espoused unpopular political beliefs, to those who practiced or advocated minority religions, to those who argued for an end to legal segregation in the South? What would have happened to criminal defendants unable to afford a lawyer, to those whose houses government officials wished to search without probable cause, to those whose property government wished to seize with little or no compensation? Under the law, what is sauce for the goose is sauce for the gander, and the same is true of the public's willingness to accept judicial decisions with which it disagrees. The rule of law is not a meal that can be ordered à la carte. Let my examples warn against taking public acceptance of the Court's authority for granted.

II

The Court as a Check

If we cannot take for granted that the public will accept the Supreme Court's decisions, how can we build or maintain a system that makes acceptance more likely? That question is particularly important where a constitution, as interpreted, gives unelected judges the power to check elected officials. This is of course the case of the US Constitution, which, as interpreted, empowers unelected judges to tell the president or Congress that a chosen action or statute violates the Constitution or other governing law.

One way of ensuring that our system increases the likelihood of public acceptance is for the Court to apply legal rules or practices that minimize the number of cases likely to provoke strong political disagreements. A brief look at what the Court does will make clear why the Court decisions that create that kind of disagreement, while important, are comparatively few in number.

For one thing, most of the cases the Court decides concern the interpretation of words in federal statutes. Does the word "costs," for example, in a statute requiring a losing party to pay an education-related lawsuit's costs, include the cost of experts that the winning party hired in the course of litigation? Members of the Court sometimes disagree about the proper interpretation of such statutes. But normally those disagreements reflect differences in methods of interpretation that are not political in nature, as I shall explain shortly. Different jurisprudential views lead to differences in result, but the outcome does not dictate the method.

Whatever labels may be applied to them, nearly all judges use the same basic interpretive tools. They will consider the statute's text, its history, relevant legal tradition, precedents, the statute's purposes (or the values that underlie it), and the relevant consequences. Different judges may tend to give different weight to one or another of these tools. Some judges place predominant weight upon text and precedent; others place greater weight on purposes and consequences. Judges may also differ about, for example, just what a statute's purpose is or just what consequences will likely flow from a particular interpretation.

These differences will only rarely have a major effect in the political realm or on the relation between Court and president. For, even if a president very much disagrees with the Court about the interpretation of a statute, the president can always ask Congress for a new law that will reflect the administration's position. In this way, disagreement is often transferred from the judicial to the political arena.

I cannot say "always," because some statutes may be difficult, if not impossible, for the political branches to change. For example, the political branches may be unable to change laws forbidding discrimination. Still, disagreements about the meaning of words in a statute *often* become (after the Court's decision) a political matter for the political branches (and not the Court) to resolve.

For another thing, many cases involving the executive branch concern the meaning and legality of regulations that the executive branch has promulgated. Some of those cases may raise important questions about the president's power. But far more often they will require the Court to determine, for example, whether the executive has followed proper administrative procedures, whether the executive has properly taken account of the views of interested citizens, or whether the justifications the executive has given for its course of action are sufficiently reasonable. A Court determination that a president's regulatory or administrative decision is unlawful will only rarely lead to serious conflict between the Court and the president, for normally the decision does not prevent the president from redoing the action, this time following proper procedures.

The Court, for example, recently found unlawful two executive branch decisions. One of the cases before the Court concerned the executive's desire to place a question about citizenship on the decennial census form. The other concerned the revocation by the president of an earlier executive branch program that allowed certain young undocumented persons to remain in the United States. The executive lost both cases in the Supreme Court. The Court nonetheless remained open to the executive deciding whether to pursue these, or similar, administrative actions again, this time lawfully following requisite administrative procedures. Thus serious disagreement between the Court and president is muted because, typically, the Court need not rule on the legality of a controversial executive branch policy, only on whether it has been lawfully imposed.

A serious conflict between Court and president is more likely to occur when the Court makes a constitutional decision; for example, when it applies to presidential actions the limitations that accompany the Constitution's highly general protections, such as "freedom of speech" or "freedom of the press," or simply "liberty." When different branches interpret these constitutional terms differently, the Court will normally have the last word. Neither the president nor Congress can lawfully change the Court's constitutional interpretations. Two features of constitutional interpretation nonetheless reduce, though they certainly do not eliminate, the risk of overt conflict even in these cases. First, the Constitution does not tell citizens what they can or cannot do. It mostly tells *governments* what they can or cannot do. The Constitution thereby sets limits confining government action. And most actions that citizens want governments to take (or not to take) fall within those limits. In this way, policing the limits, the Court is a kind of "border patrol." Given the wide scope of decision-making that the Constitution leaves to democratic political processes, only a comparatively few, though important, decisions will have the kind of major public "ballot box" effect that leads elected officials to react strongly.

Second, many constitutional questions that the Court decides concern *who* has the authority to take a particular action. For example, state government or federal government? Congress or the president? In these cases the Court's decision does not concern *whether* government can take that action at all. When the Court answers only the *who* question, it does not foreclose the desired government action but merely directs it to the right channel.

I should also note that, at one time, the Court explicitly applied a special legal doctrine called the political question doctrine. That doctrine interpreted the Constitution as prohibiting the Court from intervening in matters that were overtly political in nature, such as the drawing of the boundaries of the districts from which state legislators or members of Congress would be elected. The Court, however, later held that districts within a single state must have equal populations. In doing so, the Court eroded the force of the political question doctrine. But still the Court has avoided entering too far into what Justice Felix Frankfurter called the "political thicket," by deciding (with some exceptions) that it would not otherwise police the drawing of district boundaries.[1]

*   *   *

Despite the decision-related features that limit the risk of serious overt conflicts between Court and president, these can and do arise. Take the important

---

[1] Colegrove v. Green, 328 US 549 (1946).

example of constitutional questions about the scope of protection for basic liberties in time of war.

Again, let us hear from Cicero. He once said, *Inter arma enim silent leges,* which is commonly translated, "In times of war, the laws fall silent."[2] President Franklin D. Roosevelt's attorney general, Francis Biddle, brought this aphorism up to date during World War II when he said, "The Constitution has not greatly bothered any wartime president."[3] One might add the qualification: at least not at the time. In any case, the implication for the Court is clear: there are serious limitations upon its protective power during wartime.

During World War II, the Court considered the constitutionality of a presidential order deporting 70,000 American citizens of Japanese origin from the West Coast to camps, rather like prison camps,

[2] James A. Ballentine, *A Law Dictionary* (Indianapolis: Bobbs-Merrill, 1916), 471.

[3] Francis Biddle, *In Brief Authority* (New York: Doubleday, 1962), 219.

in intermountain regions. In *Korematsu v. United States,* the Court upheld the order by a vote of six to three.[4] Today most Americans, including most judges, believe that the majority was wrong and committed a serious injustice. Why did they reach that decision? Justice Hugo Black is said to have told the other justices at their conference in a closely related case: somebody must run this war. It is either Roosevelt or us. And we cannot.[5]

Since *Korematsu,* however, the Court's reluctance to become involved in highly sensitive war- or security-related matters has notably declined. Several years after World War II ended, the United States was again at war, this time in Korea. When the United Steel Workers threatened a strike against the big manufacturers over higher wages, President Harry S. Truman took action to ensure the uninter-

---

[4] 323 US 214 (1944).

[5] *From the Diaries of Felix Frankfurter,* ed. Joseph P. Lash (New York: Norton, 1975), 251.

rupted production of steel for the war effort. He moved to take over privately owned steel mills. But when the so-called *Youngstown Steel* case came before the Court, the majority held that the president, in the circumstances, was acting unconstitutionally.[6] Rather surprised, Truman accepted and followed the Court's decision, returning control of the mills to the owners.

One might downplay the significance of the case. President Truman was far less popular than President Roosevelt had been. The Korean War was not as galvanizing as World War II. But one cannot deny that the Court acted as if unaware of Cicero's dictum. The Court did impose a constitutional check upon the president, even in a time of war.

More recently, the Court would again abandon Cicero in four cases arising out of prisoners of war held at Guantanamo Bay in Cuba. The plaintiffs,

[6] See Youngstown Sheet & Tube Co. v. Sawyer, 343 US 579 (1952).

detained after their capture in Afghanistan at the beginning of the Global War on Terrorism, were not very popular in the United States. The defendants, including the president and the secretary of defense, were considerably more popular and certainly far more powerful. But those circumstances did not prevent the Court from deciding each of the four cases in the plaintiffs' favor. These cases included one in which the Court held unconstitutional a congressional statute denying the prisoners access to the courts.[7] The executive branch, in each case, accepted the finding. President George W. Bush said, "We'll abide by the Court's decision. That doesn't mean I have to agree with it."[8]

These, along with the earlier examples, help to illustrate an evolution in the views of presidents, branches of government, judges, and public opinion. The public now expects presidents to accept decisions

[7] See Boumediene v. Bush, 553 US 723 (2008).

[8] 44 Weekly Compilation of Presidential Documents, 830 (June 16, 2008).

of the Court, including those that are politically controversial. The Court, with no troops of its own, has reached the point of being able to impose a significant check—a legal check—upon the executive's actions, even in cases where the executive strongly disagrees with the outcome.

III

The Check and the Future

Suppose that I were to stop my account here. I would have described a history in which the American people, directly or through their elected representatives, gradually adopted the custom and habit of respecting the rule of law, even when the "law" included judicial decisions with which they strongly disagreed. The history would also be that of a Supreme Court that gradually expanded its authority to protect an individual's basic constitutional rights, even during a time of war. I would certainly not claim that this history's theme has always been one of progress, for the United States, including its judicial system, has had many ups and downs. Those downs include slavery, a civil war, segregation, and court decisions such as *Dred Scott v. Sandford* and the Japanese internment cases to name only a few.[1] Still, at the

[1] 60 US 393 (1857).

Fig. 1: Percent who have a ____view of the Supreme Court

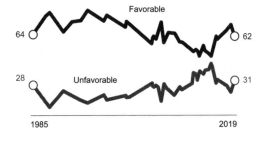

end of it all, the public has accepted a rule of law. And so far, the public seems to have maintained its confidence in the Court. A Pew Research poll showed, for example, that in 2019 62 percent of Americans held a favorable opinion of the Court, about the same percentage as in 1985.

However much I might like to tell this story, I cannot, for matters are not that simple. Nor is the future ever certain. We cannot now know what historians in years to come will write about the public's acceptance of the Court, let alone the rule of law.

Are there significant features of American society that threaten the continued acceptance of a rule of law, at least insofar as judicial decisions embody, and explicate, that law? To my mind, there are at least two threats that present cause for concern. First, we see a growing public suspicion and distrust of all government institutions. Pew reports that in 1958, 73 percent of Americans trusted the federal government's decisions most of the time. By 2019 that number had fallen to just 19 percent.

At the same time, we have seen a gradual change in the way the media, along with other institutions that comment upon the law, understand and represent the judicial institution. Journalists' understanding is important, for it is only through their reporting that the vast majority of Americans learns just what courts, including the Supreme Court, do. Several decades ago, few if any of these reporters and

Fig. 2: Percent who trust the government in Washington always or most of the tim

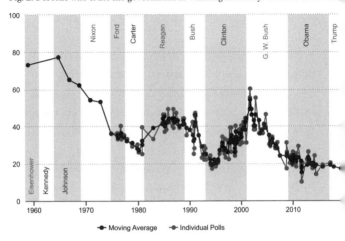

commentators, when reporting a decision, would have mentioned the name or political party of the president who had nominated a judge to office. Today the media do so as a matter of course. Going further, they systematically label judges as conservative or liberal. Likewise, the Senate confirmation process has changed over the past two or three decades, becoming

50

more starkly partisan. Where not long ago a qualified candidate could enjoy broad bipartisan support, recent confirmations have become essentially party-line votes. Senators will often describe a nominee they oppose as too liberal or too conservative, and thus "outside the mainstream." What senators say, reported by the press to their constituents, reinforces the view that politics, not legal merits, drives Supreme Court decisions.

Thus the popular perception has grown that Supreme Court justices are unelected political officials or "junior varsity" politicians themselves, rather than jurists. But that is not how most judges see themselves or the judiciary. Nevertheless, it has become a matter of concern that this is what the public thinks.

As I have said, I believe that jurisprudential differences, not political ones, account for most, perhaps almost all, of judicial disagreements. At least, that is what I have come to think, having worked at the Court over many years. But let me explain in somewhat greater detail why I believe that "political" is the wrong word to describe even the more controversial court decisions.

*   *   *

When I hear the word "political," I think of my work on the staff of the Senate Judiciary Committee. We staffers would sometimes play a kind of game, imagining that Senator Edward Kennedy, the committee chair, simultaneously received two calls, one from the secretary of the interior, another from the mayor of Worcester, Massachusetts. Which would he answer first? Most of us would bet on the mayor. Why? Because many of the senator's constituents lived in Worcester. That, in a sense, is politics. Who elected you? Are you a Democrat or a Republican? Which position is more popular? Where are the votes?

Politics in this elemental sense is not present at the Court.

But what about ideology, as apart from partisanship? Are you an Adam Smith "free enterpriser"? Are you a Marxist? To what ideology do you, as an individual, tend to subscribe? This is a tougher question, because we all have our predispositions. But if I catch myself headed toward deciding a case on the basis of some general ideological commitment, I know I have gone down the wrong path, and I correct course. My colleagues think the same way. All studiously try to avoid deciding cases on the basis of ideology rather than law. And my experience is that this is true of judges as a group, whether they serve on the Supreme Court or any other court.

Why then do political groups so strongly support some persons for appointment to the Court and so strongly oppose others? I have come to believe that such groups typically confuse perceived personal ideology (inferred from party affiliation or that of the nominating executive) and professed judicial philosophy. Doing so, political groups often support individuals who hold a particular judicial philosophy, imagining that it will reliably lead to results that favor the group's political outlook.

Will a judge who places major interpretive weight upon the law's literal text, for example, over time come to legal conclusions that we can characterize as more conservative? Some think so, but I tend to think: perhaps. Perhaps not. It depends upon the case. Political groups may favor a particular appointment, but once appointed a judge naturally decides a case in the way that he or she believes the law demands. It is a judge's sworn duty to be impartial, and all of us take that oath seriously. That may disappoint those who made the appointment, and often it does, sometimes maddeningly. President Theodore Roosevelt once said of his appointee Oliver Wendell Holmes Jr., when the justice rendered a decision that the president thought was wrong, "I could carve a judge with more backbone out of a banana."[2] In a word, no matter what a political partisan believes will happen after his or her preferred judge is appointed, that judge, once on the bench, decides according to what he or she believes the law requires.

[2] Edmund Morris, *Theodore Rex* (New York: Random House, 2001), 316.

But why then are decisions of particular judges so predictable? Why are there "alignments" of the same judges on the same side of various controversial cases? Alignments normally reflect similar judicial philosophies. Alignments also may reflect similar views as to the meaning and comparative importance of particular constitutional provisions. As I said earlier, some judges emphasize text and history; some emphasize purposes and consequences. Some see parts of the First Amendment as more intimately tied to government's basic democratic structure than do others. Such factors, key in almost every case, can explain alignments and predictability far more readily and cogently than one can with reference to politics. If political groups support, or a president appoints, a justice whose jurisprudential philosophy will, they believe, advance some political agenda in the long run, so be it. To a judge, that would seem a recipe for frustration. Judicial philosophy is not a code word for politics.

But I must hesitate. I want to qualify what I just wrote.

For one thing, the cases that come before our Court are typically difficult calls, with considerable merit on both sides. And the key legal text relevant to a decision is often a constitutional text using such highly general words as "liberty" or "the freedom of speech." Within broad limits those words do not dictate their own content. Where a matter is open in this way, a judge's background, experience, and personal views about the law's objectives, the Court's role, or the nation's life can make a difference. Does it matter that I grew up in San Francisco in the 1950s, that I went to a public high school, that I studied at Stanford, that I have led the life I have lived? Of course it matters. I cannot jump out of my own skin. No one can. And by the time one reaches middle age, he or she normally has "views"—about a profession, about this nation, and so on. Those views, sometimes too general even to articulate, can play a role in a difficult, close case. But the fact that judges on our Court may have somewhat different general perspectives and experiences is hardly a bad thing in a nation of 330 million people of every race, religion, national origin, and point of view.

For another thing, politics is not just about voting for a particular candidate or a particular legislative agenda. It is also about basic political philosophy. And it is sometimes difficult to separate what counts as a jurisprudential view from what counts as political philosophy, which, in turn, can shape views of policy. A judge, for example, might believe strongly in federalism or free markets or government regulation of business. Indeed, he or she might believe that the Constitution works well for this nation precisely because it embodies one of those basic views. Are those views jurisprudential, or are they a form of political philosophy? Hard to say. To what extent do these political or jurisprudential views shape judges' perspectives on policies at issue in particular cases? Yet harder to say.

Further, while the Court's decisions, seen at a highly general level, do tend to reflect certain major changes in the political world, they do so only slowly, with changes in Court doctrine coming long after changes in politics. Consider the New Deal and the major changes it made in the role of government, particularly the federal government. Eventually the

Court modified and reshaped its case law, particularly its constitutional case law, to account for, and adapt to, these changes. But the Court was transformed only after the retirements of several older judges and the appointments of new judges by New Deal presidents Franklin D. Roosevelt and Harry S. Truman. The next wave of judges likely thought they were replacing outworn and incorrect legal principles with sounder new ones. These judges likely thought that they were following the Constitution's basic intent to create a workable form of democratic government that would last hundreds of years. But it is difficult to deny that the Court's overall approaches reflect to a degree the shift in political views of a majority of this nation's citizens.

One could argue that it is a good thing that the country's jurisprudential principles evolve in this way, every few decades, to reflect new generations and changing circumstances. Jefferson likely thought so. But that kind of change does connect jurisprudence with politics. At the least, separating the jurisprudential from the political aspects, or causes, of this slow change is not an easy task.

AND THE PERIL OF POLITICS

Finally, judges may appear to be engaged in politics when in fact they are taking stock of institutional considerations. For example, the Court properly pays attention to those considerations every time it refuses to hear a case on the ground that the justices are unlikely to be able to provide legal guidance that will help the lower courts. But sometimes those considerations border on the political, particularly when they temper, or depart from, important practices well embedded in the task of judges.

Consider one such practice. Judges should not, and virtually never do, pay particular attention to public opinion. They must decide cases on legal grounds, not on the basis of what is popular. But why do I qualify what I just wrote with a word like "virtually"? Why not "absolutely never"? Go back to *Brown v. Board of Education.* The Court was properly concerned that the South would not follow its holding requiring racial integration. Irrespective of what the Court said, states might refuse to end legal racial segregation. For quite a few years after rendering its decision, the Court carefully chose which cases to take, sometimes avoiding ones that might thwart its ambitions in *Brown*—for example, those that asked the Court to set aside laws forbidding interracial marriages. Eventually, in *Loving v. Virginia*, the Court did set aside those laws.[3] The thirteen-year delay between *Brown* and *Loving*, a calculated part of the Court's enforcement strategy, reflected its views about the state of public opinion. One could well claim that here the Court had entered the realm of politics. Or was it merely protecting its invaluable institutional authority? It is hard to say.

Remember Justice Black's remark at a Court conference in a case related to *Korematsu*: in effect he said that somebody must run this war. It is either Roosevelt or us. And we cannot. That view produced a terrible result. But what about the statement itself? Was it purely legal, or did it reflect politics to some degree? Again, hard to say.

The present Court is often described as having a conservative majority. And the Court's decision in the 2000 presidential election case, *Bush v. Gore*, is

[3] 388 US 1 (1967).

often referred to as an example of its bias in favor of conservative causes. On the other hand, the Court refused to hear or decide cases grounded in the political disagreements arising out of the 2020 election between Donald Trump and Joe Biden.[4] The Court did uphold the constitutionality of Obamacare, the health care program favored by liberals.[5] It did reaffirm precedents that favored a woman's right to an abortion.[6] It did find unlawful certain immigration, census, and other orders, rules, or regulations promulgated by a conservative president.[7] But at the same time the Court made other decisions that can reasonably be understood as favoring

---

[4] See, for example, Texas v. Pennsylvania, 592 US __ (2020).

[5] See NFIB v. Sebelius, 567 US 519 (2012).

[6] See June Med. Servs. v. Russo, 591 US __ (2020).

[7] See, for example, Department of Homeland Security v. Regents of the University of California, 591 US __ (2020).

conservative policy objectives and disfavoring liberal ones.

These inconsistencies convince me that it is wrong to think of the Court as a political institution. And it is doubly wrong to think of its members as junior varsity politicians. But, given 1) the highly general language of the Constitution; 2) the ambiguous connections among jurisprudence, political philosophy, and policy; and 3) the inevitable, conscious or unconscious, impact of an individual's background upon his or her basic views of the world, to suggest a total and clean divorce between the Court and politics is not quite right either.

It may be accurate, even if insufficient, to say a judge would naturally think that his or her legal reasoning and decision making has no relationship to politics. Or a judge may believe that any relationship between politics and his or her jurisprudence is, at the very least, highly nuanced. But that is not the impression the public has lately received. And if the public is growing to believe the contrary of what judges believe, we should not be surprised if political parties, too, see the nomination of a judge as simply an opportunity to extend their political influence. Nor should we be surprised if proposals for structural change of the Court become a topic of general public concern. But structural change represents a temptation better resisted. For if the public comes to see judges as merely "politicians in robes," its confidence in the courts, and in the rule of law itself, can only decline. With that, the Court's authority can only decline, too, including its hard-won power to act as a constitutional check on the other branches. Thus a short-term victory in the great zero-sum game that our politics has become could bring about grave structural damage not only to an essential constitutional institution but also to our system of government.

What, then, can we do to stop the attrition of confidence? Let me sketch a few thoughts about what judges themselves might do inside the Court as well as what I believe others might do outside it, in our broader society.

THE AUTHORITY OF THE COURT

What can we do, we judges of the Supreme Court, to help maintain the confidence and respect both of others in government and of the public in general? How can the Court preserve the authority it has gradually obtained over the course of time?

Again, as Hamilton pointed out, we have neither purse nor sword. We cannot easily reward or frighten our fellow citizens. To obtain their respect, we must rely upon making decisions that reflect both practical wisdom and justice. I would emphasize five features of our work that express this aspiration and that judges normally try to keep in mind.

Just Do the Job

Do not seek or expect popularity. The job of constitutional judges is to interpret or to apply the legal phrases that we find either in a statute or in the Constitution itself. Because the cases that we hear normally concern instances in which lower-court judges have differed over the same legal question, the scope of the words, their meaning in context, and their application is typically uncertain.

As I have said, judges have several tools available to help them with this interpretive work: the ordinary sense of words, history, tradition, precedents, purposes (or values that underlie a constitutional provision), and consequences related to those purposes. Judges vary as to how they apportion emphasis among these various considerations, but virtually every judge will use each of these as tools on one occasion or another.

Any appellate judge's work then consists of reading briefs (and other papers), listening to oral arguments, attentively following discussions between judges and lawyers, discussing cases with colleagues, writing draft opinions, submitting those opinions to colleagues for views and criticism, and releasing opinions to the public along with any concurring or dissenting opinions of colleagues. The decision-making process does not, and should not, consider popularity, support, criticism, or the likely reactions of business groups, labor groups, or the media. The most those not parties to a case can do is to present their arguments directly to the Court, usually in the form of an amicus curiae brief. The justices may consider these briefs relevant insofar as they offer expertise or insight that translates into legal arguments. But nothing should interfere with a judge's impartially discharging his or her duties, in accordance with the judicial oath of office.

My experience from more than thirty years as a judge has shown me that anyone taking the judicial oath takes it very much to heart. A judge's loyalty is to the rule of law, not the political party that helped to secure his or her appointment.

Clarity

For a Supreme Court justice, clarity is not simply a question of good manners. Clarity in writing is a professional necessity. It shows a clarity of thought. Clarity helps convince the reader that the judge has decided the case according to reason and the law, not according to politics or caprice.

At the same time, we must keep in mind the nature of the audience that will take particular interest in a decision. A bankruptcy case, for example, will have a more technical readership than one about freedom of expression. An opinion that will have a broad public audience requires writing that is simpler and more direct than does an opinion about bankruptcy.

Deliberation

Deliberation, as others have said, is not conversation, much less gossip, praise, or indignation. Deliberation has a particular sort of goal: to reach a decision. For a group of judges, such as our Court's justices, deliberation involves weighing the arguments for and against different possible interpretations or applications of a legal phrase with the goal of arriving at a decision.

It is tempting to note that there is a basic difference in the kind of deliberation undertaken by political officials (or by ordinary people) and by judges.

The first kind, one might say, concerns an action to be undertaken; the second concerns the justice of an action that already has been undertaken. A judge, Aristotle thought, "evaluates the justice of past actions."

The distinction may help to characterize the work of some appellate judges, as judicial opinions typically do weigh the justice of past actions, including prior judicial findings. But there is a way in which this tidy distinction is less helpful as applied to the Supreme Court, particularly inasmuch as its decisions will help determine the confidence that the public has, or will maintain, in the judicial institution itself. For while decisions about, say, the lawfulness of abortions or of a gay person's right to work without discrimination rest upon analysis of prior fact and law, these decisions nonetheless have more to do with the future than with the past. Recall once more the challenge of, on the one hand, implementing integration, while, on the other, satisfying the legal need to ensure that the phrase "equal protection of the laws" is meaningful. How could the Court have done the latter without taking full account of the consequences of its *Brown* decision, along with the importance of successful implementation? This kind of problem, infrequent though it may be, helps explain the legal need to consider consequences. But the result is that, because the Court must in part look to the future, opponents of its decision may argue that it is acting like a legislature, not a court.

When deciding this kind of question, as with other legal decisions, judges draw upon their own jurisprudential views of proper interpretation and perhaps of the nature of law or of the Court itself. Different basic views can lead to differences of opinion among judges as to proper outcome. But the future is nonetheless at issue.

How does this deliberation work in practice? Oral arguments can help a justice make up his or her mind. Moreover, the questions a justice asks at oral argument will sometimes help other justices understand his or her approach to the case as well as the difficulties he or she may have with particular

proposed solutions. Ordinarily, however, deliberation among the justices begins at conference, held
once or twice each week. There, the justices will discuss the cases more formally, and they will try to
arrive at preliminary conclusions.

The conferences are confidential. Only the justices
participate. Each justice, in turn, presents his or her
point of view, and then there may be responses and
more general discussion. The discussion is rarely
completely open or far-ranging. Normally a justice's
point of view rests upon the individual use he or she
makes of the tools I previously mentioned (text, history, tradition, precedents, purposes or values, and
consequences). Normally each justice arrives at the
conference with a point of view while remaining
open to the possibility that it will change. Perhaps
the most difficult part of a deliberation for a justice
is not formulating a point of view as much as it is
demonstrating a capacity to change that point of
view when faced with the persuasive views of others.

The success of a deliberation overall may depend
upon a cliché: listen to others. When I worked in the

Senate on Senator Kennedy's staff, I learned one method that can be very helpful in bringing together those who deliberate. When someone sets forth a point of view, you can ask him to explain it in more detail. When he does so, often he will mention a few things, perhaps only details, with which you agree. You can then suggest that you work with that agreement and see whether it will provide a basis for broader agreement. Often it does. The senator used to remind his staff, "Do not worry about who gets the credit. Credit is a weapon. If you reach agreement, there will be enough credit to go around; and, if you fail, who wants the credit?" Certainly, the Court is not the Senate; nor is it a political institution. Nonetheless, this advice remains relevant.

Compromise

Because a judge's decision rests upon principle, it is often difficult for a judge to compromise. Many foreign courts issue only a single opinion in a case, without published dissent; compromise, then, being entirely necessary, may, through force of habit, become easier to reach. But the American system finds its origins in that of England, where each judge would present his own opinion, giving his own reasons for reaching a particular result. In the United States we have taken something of a middle course.

I doubt that a unanimity requirement would work well in this country. At least it would not tend to make the pubic believe that the Court was always unanimous. Rather, many would think that disagreements remain but are hidden. And that attitude would not increase trust in the Court. Regardless, our system allows published dissents. And a draft dissent will sometimes, though not often, lead a tentative majority to change its mind, altering the outcome. More typically, a dissent leads a judge writing for a majority to improve that opinion in light of the criticisms that a draft dissent makes.

Although members of our Court can write dissenting and concurring opinions, in the end, they must still produce one opinion that at least five can join. There must be one opinion "for the Court," to guide the public. And that often means that compromise is necessary.

There are different ways to reach a compromise. First, let us consider the use of approaches that we can group together under the term "minimalism." Cass Sunstein has carefully analyzed this approach, emphasizing that it can consist of deciding a case on narrow grounds (when broader grounds are available), deciding it with reduced emphasis upon the basic jurisprudential principles that underlie it, or deciding it using some combination of these two methods.

Deciding a case on narrower grounds can serve several different purposes. Consider, for example, the well-accepted practice of resting a decision, if at all possible, upon the interpretation of a statute rather than the Constitution. That practice in part reflects the difficulty of changing an erroneous interpretation of the Constitution—that is, of enacting a constitutional amendment. Congress, however, can far more easily change what it believes to be an undesirable interpretation of a statute: it can far more easily enact a new statute than the nation can enact a constitutional amendment.

To take another example, suppose that the Court must decide whether police needed to have a warrant to search Verizon's cell phone communications-tower records in order to see where a suspect (the cell phone owner) was at a particular time. Does it matter that the police had already observed the suspect in a public place at the time in question—say, a street in front of a grocery store? Or should the Court decide more broadly, writing that the Fourth Amendment requires, or does not require, a warrant regardless?

The fact that the ubiquity of cell phone technology is relatively new can make a difference. That is because Americans decide in complex ways how new technologies affect old values. Consider, for example, the present arguments surrounding free speech and the internet. As Tocqueville pointed out, Americans will surround such questions with a "clamor" of debate. Different groups (law enforcement, civil liberties organizations, the press, state or local officials, academics, and many others) will take different positions. Legislatures will have hearings. Different agencies or local governments may try different solutions. The Court, in my view, often understands less about the relevant possibilities and consequences than do others. If so, the Court would do best to weigh in last—after other parts of government have reached statutory or regulatory solutions. The Court can then determine whether the solutions that others have reached democratically fall within the broad limits that the Constitution sets. In such circumstances, the Court is often well-advised to keep interim decisions narrow lest it prematurely restrict the arena in which more democratic forces are at play.

When technology is new, the Court will often take a minimalist approach. To take one of many possible examples: in the recent case *Packingham v. North Carolina,* the Court considered for nearly the first time the relation between criminal law's fairness requirements and the modern internet. Specifically, the Court considered a state law that prohibited previously convicted sex offenders from visiting websites on which minors were known to be active. The Court did not enunciate a general principle that might apply well beyond the specific state statute. Rather the Court held that the statute was too broad, while also pointing out that this finding "should not be interpreted as barring a State from enacting more specific laws than the one at issue."[8]

One purpose, relevant here, often served by minimalist approaches is to produce a compromise that can be the basis of a majority opinion, which at least five justices will join, perhaps bringing together justices considered conservative and justices considered liberal. Suppose, for example, that the Court is to decide a case involving state laws that require family planning centers, including religiously affiliated ones, to inform clients about how they can obtain an abortion. The case might involve complex issues of constitutional law, including free speech, religious freedom, and abortion rights. And suppose further that the lower courts have declined to decide a

[8] 582 US __ (2017).

related issue whose resolution might obviate the need to answer the constitutional questions. A minimalist approach might be to simply remand the case to the lower courts so that they can first decide that related issue. The Supreme Court decision might seem extremely narrow—focusing almost exclusively upon the individual case—and it might seem extremely shallow, saying next to nothing about underlying constitutional jurisprudence. But the Court's decision might bring together five or more justices, while leaving them free to assert their (different) underlying constitutional views on another day or in another case.

Consider another example in which the Court took a minimalist approach, the 2014 case *Bond v. United States*. The Chemical Weapons Convention sets forth a broad definition of forbidden use of a chemical weapon. Congress enacted that definition into law, in the form of a criminal statute. The federal government prosecuted and convicted Carol Anne Bond for violating that statute by dusting a skin-irritating chemical on the doorknob of a house of a certain woman whom she disliked. (The woman was having an affair with Bond's husband.) The case might have led the Court to determine whether the Constitution sets certain limits upon the president's power to enter into treaties or upon Congress's power to implement treaties. But the Court decided the case narrowly, simply holding that Congress had not intended the statute to reach run-of-the-mill assault cases such as Bond's. That narrow holding drew broad acquiescence among judges who, perhaps, held different views about the larger constitutional questions.[9]

I do not say that compromise is always desirable or that minimalism always is either. After all, I have written opinions for the Court in highly controversial abortion cases, cases that the Court decided five to four. In those cases I believed that neither minimalism nor compromise was in order. Moreover, the most momentous decisions resist minimalism. In *Brown v. Board of Education,* the Court's holding

[9] 572 US 844 (2014).

was broad, not narrow; deep, not shallow. And that opinion was both necessary and helpful to the nation. I say only that minimalism will sometimes quite properly help the Court find a majority, perhaps more than a simple majority, by allowing judges who hold different views on the broader legal questions to come together in answering narrower ones.

A narrow decision is not the only form of compromise. There are also more direct forms. A justice can sometimes "swallow" a dissenting view. She might decide, for example, to join a majority opinion with which she disagrees, perhaps noting that she is doing so only to create a majority opinion needed for guidance in the particular case. One can write a dissenting opinion or memorandum and not publish it. One can decide not to have one's view about granting a certiorari petition revealed to the public. I can refrain from writing a concurring opinion that would otherwise set out just where and how I agree or disagree with the majority's view. In most of these instances, the decision *not* to dissent gives a public impression of greater unanimity than actually exists.

When should a judge prove willing to compromise? Each judge must look to his or to her own conscience to find an answer to that question. But, in doing so, a judge must take two general factors into consideration. For one, the judge should ask, who is the primary audience for the decision: other judges, lawyers, the general public? Is that audience more likely to need to know the position of the Court, or is it interested in the individual opinions of different judges?

Moreover, there is only one Constitution of the United States. There is not a "Constitution according to Justice Scalia" or a "Constitution according to Justice O'Connor" or according to any other individual judge. It is what the Court decides, not what individual justices think, that typically matters most. The presence of too many dissenting opinions risks diminishing the public's confidence in Court decisions. Many European courts, as I have said, do not issue dissenting opinions, and it is primarily for that reason.

Why is it difficult to find compromise? In some cases, a judge will find that principle or conscience prevents him or her from agreeing with a particular view. Consider, for example, a case where compromise might seem possible: a state's rules designed to contain the spread of serious disease (say, COVID-19) forbid churches to have services inside, but not outside, the church building. Why wouldn't all members of the Court be able to agree that a state can limit indoor attendance, as long as it doesn't forbid services entirely? Many might believe that freedom of religion must yield a bit to scientific consensus at times of significant risks to public health. But the answer could be that some judges believe that the state must be especially careful when imposing restrictions upon religious worship. If an individual judge believes strongly enough in either of these competing principles—that freedom of religion is overriding, or that accommodations should be made to the demands of a public health crisis—and that belief is so strong that, as a matter of conscience, he or she simply cannot join the other side, the Court will have to issue several different opinions rather than one compromise opinion.

This kind of conscience-related problem can arise even in what seems a more technically oriented case. Consider the following: Congress enacted a statute requiring cable companies to carry over-the-air television stations. A cable company argued that the statute violated its free speech rights. Four members of the Court thought that the statute was valid because it served a valid antitrust purpose. Four members thought the statute was not valid because it did *not* serve a valid antitrust purpose. One judge believed that the statute did not serve a valid antitrust purpose but also believed that Congress could enact it anyway. The latter judge wrote a separate concurring opinion stating just that. The separate opinion meant that the majority's opinion, upholding the statute, lacked a majority rationale. This was a real case, *Turner Broadcasting Systems, Inc. v. Federal Communications Commission*.[10] I was, in fact, the judge who wrote that separate opinion. So why did I write it? Probably because, having taught antitrust law for

[10] 520 US 180 (1997).

many years, I found it too difficult to accept an antitrust rationale that I thought was wrong. My opinion might have been an example of what Justice Holmes once called a "can't help." A judge's conscience will not allow him to join an opinion that he thinks goes too far. What counts as too far may depend upon the background of the individual judge. And the conscience-related problem is not always readily apparent to the public.

Similarly a judge who has previously expressed a view, even on a fairly minor technical matter, may hesitate to join fully a majority opinion expressing a contrary view on the minor matter, lest the legal public think that the judge is being inconsistent (or has changed his mind). The judge may well feel obliged to write a concurring opinion, even in a case where the appearance of disagreement is undesirable. The existence of that concurring opinion reflects the importance of personal consistency, and not only to the individual. Personal consistency matters to the institution because it reflects the judge's obligation to follow his or her view of what the law demands.

Consistency demonstrates that judges are not free to decide cases any way they wish, or any way that might seem convenient, on a particular day.

A judge joins, or suggests an inclination to join, an opinion by sending a memorandum to the writing judge. That memorandum typically lists changes that the sender would like to see the writer make. Of course, suggesting too many changes or changes that are too minor can work against the possibility of compromise. All recognize that an appellate court, having reached a tentative decision, must delegate discretion to the writing judge as to just what words will be committed to paper. The question is how much discretion.

As my examples suggest, there are no hard-and-fast rules telling a judge when, or how much, to compromise. Too little compromise risks substitution of an individual judge's views for the views of—and the law set forth by—a court. On the other hand, were there never, or only rarely, a dissenting opinion, the public would begin to doubt the sincerity of decisions. The discerning public is aware of the jurisprudential differences among judges and could lose faith in holdings that do not reflect the judicial diversity they have come to expect.

In either circumstance—too much compromise or too little—the public's confidence in the Court itself, as a legitimate interpreter of laws, is undermined. Where do we find the happy medium? That is a conscience-based decision that each judge has to make. But let me add that the more diverse the jurisprudential views on a court, the more important compromise among the judges becomes.

Broader Perspective

Consider the minority of cases that address important and deeply held social or political beliefs, such as the right to an abortion or to the freedom of religion. These cases often concern far more than technical legal issues. These cases also touch upon deeply engrained customs, habits, and practices. Thus, a large part of the American public takes more than a passing interest in what the Court decides. How should the Court decide that kind of case?

Justices in such a case begin in the usual way: they read the briefs, hear oral arguments, and meet and discuss the case in conference. Then they gather the raw materials—textual analysis, history, tradition, precedents, and so forth—which, when transformed, become a judgment. As I suggested earlier, that judgment is only to a minor extent a judgment about what has happened in the past. Rather, the decision is more an instruction, with respect to law and judicial action, aimed at the future. And, unlike much of the justices' work, the decision does not simply concern the actions or means for bringing about an agreed-upon ultimate end. The decision in a controversial case involving deeply held values often brings into question the nature of the ultimate end that the judge or justice must seek.

Where are justices and judges to find those ends, those ultimate objectives, that must guide them as they transform their raw material? Judges find these ends in the Constitution itself. In particular, they find them in the values that underlie that document and its provisions. That is what those who speak of the

Constitution's "spirit" normally mean. The racial integration that the Court demanded in *Brown v. Board of Education*, for example, is not simply a logical conclusion drawn from the constitutional provision that insists upon "equal protection of the laws." Ruling in favor of integration is also an affirmation of the value that underlies the equal-protection provision; the ruling is an affirmation of justice itself.

Judges can sometimes find that the framers' determination to write a Constitution that would prove *workable* itself provides an ultimate end that can help resolve individual cases. I suspect that the Court opinions seeking to end segregation in the South, as well as those that ratified New Deal efforts to create different kinds of federal government–related institutions, reflect this ultimate objective as well.

But let me provide more specific examples of the way in which underlying constitutional purposes can inform ultimate interpretive ends. Unlike some nations, the United States does not maintain an absolute commitment to secularism. Rather, two provisions of the Constitution govern the relation of religion and public life. One of them forbids prohibition of "the free exercise" of religion. The other prohibits the enactment of laws "respecting the establishment of religion." These provisions, for example, allow Congress to open its sessions with a prayer, but they forbid government from subsidizing religious training. It is far from obvious how the provisions apply to religious monuments placed on public property, say, the government's placing the Tablets of the Law (that is, the Ten Commandments) on the grounds of the Texas State Capitol or on the walls of a Kentucky state court. The Supreme Court had to decide this last question. And, in my view, doing so required the Court to look to the primary objectives of the religion clauses.

The clauses in part reflect a compromise made in seventeenth-century England, which helped put an end to the Wars of Religion. In essence, that compromise said, "You are free to practice your religion and teach it to your children, and I am free to do the same." The goal then, as now, was to minimize social conflicts growing out of religion. It is essential to reach that goal in the United States, where adherents of many different religions must live together. When trying to find an answer to the specific legal questions of religious monuments, I thought it necessary to put considerable weight upon this ultimate objective of the religion clauses.

Take another example, one related to the constitutional guarantee of free speech. That guarantee is necessary in a representative democracy, for it allows the public to develop and to transmit to those whom they elect different thoughts, ideas, criticisms, and points of view. Free-speech protection helps to guarantee "a marketplace of ideas" and a "transmission belt" that carries expression from the individual to her community and, eventually, to her elected representatives. Reference to both of these basic purposes—production and dissemination of ideas—can help resolve difficult legal questions. Why, for example, does the Court interpret the constitutional term "free speech" more strictly 1) when a government rule or regulation limits the scope of the marketplace of ideas or the transmission belt than 2) when a government rule or regulation limits the scope of speech as part of, say, ordinary economic or commercial regulation? In the first instance, free speech protects necessary elements of a workable democracy; in the second, one considers, for example, the economic or social government regulation that democratic processes have helped to bring about. That is a good reason for interpreting the First Amendment as applying more strictly to the first kind of restriction than to the second.

I could say more about the examples. They are controversial in their details. But I use them only to suggest that reference to basic underlying constitutional purposes can help answer difficult interpretive questions. Because the Constitution itself seeks to establish a workable democracy, to protect basic human rights, and to help hold together a highly diverse society, reference to those purposes also moves Court decisions in the direction of Justice (with a capital "J"). And it is in this way, not in seeking popularity with one group or another, that the Court can preserve, perhaps augment, public confidence in its authority.

OUTSIDE THE COURT

What can people outside the Court do to help maintain the public's confidence in the Court and the law's authority? As I said in response to the Ghanaian chief justice's questions, a nation's willingness to follow the law and to respect the courts is a matter of custom and habit. Those habits include a willingness to follow judicial decisions with which you disagree, that may affect you adversely, and that may be wrong. After all, in a five-to-four decision, some judges must be wrong.

I routinely observe Americans' willingness to respect the Court's authority, and how that willingness helps keep our nation together. I keep in mind the fact that we are a nation of nearly 330 million, with people of every race, every religion, many different national origins, and virtually every conceivable point of view. I regularly see from the bench these highly diverse groups of people trying to work out their differences through law, rather than in more brutal ways. I then understand the framers' hope that the Constitution would last and become a national treasure.

What can we do to maintain this habit, this custom, this treasure? Judges and lawyers cannot succeed at this alone. Rather, the 329 million Americans who are not lawyers or judges must understand the need to maintain that habit, and they must accept it. We need to explain it to our children and to our grandchildren, hoping that they too will understand its importance.

When I describe to students what I believe we can do, I emphasize three general efforts. The first, and most obvious, concerns *education*. Future generations must understand how our government works. They need to know that they are, and will be, part of that government. They need to understand what the rule of law is and how, from the time of King John and Magna Carta, it has offered protection against government action that is arbitrary, capricious, autocratic, or tyrannical. Not too long ago, nearly every high school student would take a class in civics, where they would learn this and more. Today, many schools do not even teach the subject as such. A 2014 study, for example, showed that only 23 percent of American eighth graders were proficient in civics.[11] As for American adults, in 2016, only one in four could name the three branches of the federal government.[12] This is not just a pity. If we hope to maintain our democracy, lack of civics knowledge is a disaster. Justice Sandra Day O'Connor worked hard with an organization called iCivics to help correct this deficiency. Like her and many others,

---

[11] See "2014 Civics Assessment," National Center for Education Statistics, http://www.nationsreportcard .gov/hgc_2014/#civics.

[12] Rebecca Winthrop, "The Need for Civic Education in 21st-Century Schools," Brookings Institution, June 4, 2020, http://www.brookings.edu/policy2020 /bigideas/the-need-for-civic-education-in-21st -century-school.

I believe we must return to the teaching of civics. We can do so in a way that does not ignore or excuse such evils as structural efforts to perpetuate racial discrimination. Our history, though tainted, is not the negation of our constitutional ideals; it is rather a complicated history with advances and setbacks. It takes place in the complicated context of our labors, past and current, to try to embody those ideals in working institutions.

The second effort concerns *participation* in the public life of a nation with a highly diverse population and that rests upon a rule of law. There are many different ways to participate in public life. One can serve on a school board, a library committee, an arts council. One can participate in a neighborhood improvement project, help teach children to read, work for the improvement of parks and playgrounds. One can vote, campaign, run for office. The possibilities are endless.

In some respects, however, the possibilities for participation have declined. As school districts consolidated, the number of school boards fell from about 84,000 in 1950 to about 13,500 in 2016.[13] The number of jury trials has declined as well. In New York State, for example, over the last twenty-five years the number of jury trials is down by 50 percent, from about 40,000 to about 20,000.[14] Depending on the case, that trend may have helped or hurt countless individuals and groups who were parties to cases that went untried, but the effect in the aggregate has also been to reduce the opportunity for ordinary citizens to participate in, and to understand, the role they are meant to play in our justice

---

[13] Lawrence W. Kenny and Amy B. Schmidt, "The Decline in the Number of School Districts in the U.S.: 1950–1980," *Public Choice* 79, no. 1–2 (1994): 1–18; Daarel Burnette II, "Consolidation Push Roils Vermont Landscape," *Education Week,* February 16, 2016, http://www.edweek.org/policy -politics/consolidation-push-roils-vermont -landscape/2016/02.

[14] Benjamin Weiser, "Jury Trials Vanish, and Justice Is Served behind Closed Doors," *New York Times,* August 7, 2016, A1.

system. And, of course, others have written at length about the social cost of too much time spent surfing the internet, engaging in activities that separate you from public life.[15]

When speaking to students, I add that my imploring them to participate in public life grows out of my daily work with the Constitution. That document foresees their participation. Without it, the Constitution, and the democratic system of government that it creates, will not work. For without democratic participation, understanding is limited, and with little understanding there can be little confidence. My hope and belief is that the effort of participation will lead, through the understanding it promotes, to greater confidence in government, including the Court.

[15] See, for example, Richard Wike and Alexandra Castillo, "Many around the World Are Disengaged from Politics," Pew Research Center, October 17, 2018, http://www.pewresearch.org/global/2018/10/17/international-political-engagement.

The third effort concerns *practice*. The Constitution creates methods for resolving differences through participation, through argument and debate, through free speech, through a free press, and through compromise. Students and adults alike must practice the skills of cooperation and compromise to learn them and to keep them.

Few Americans were better or more experienced practitioners of cooperation and compromise than was Benjamin Franklin. Here is what he said to convince the Constitutional Convention to adopt the Constitution itself:

> I agree to this Constitution, with all its faults . . . I doubt too whether any other convention we can obtain, may be able to make a better Constitution: For when you assemble a number of men to have the advantage of their joint wisdom, you inevitably assemble with those men all their prejudices, their passions, their errors of opinion, their local interests, and their selfish views. From such an assembly can a perfect production be

expected? . . . I consent, sir, to this Constitution because I expect no better, and
because I am not sure that it is not the best.
The opinions I have had of its errors I sacri-
fice to the public good.[16]

Here we see cooperation and compromise not as cyn-
ical expediency, as some nowadays decry it, but as
the embodiment of the democratic ideal.

When I hear students lament the divisions within
our country as too deep, I ask them to remember
the constitutional need for participation, for argument, for deliberation, for efforts to convince others,
for voting, all of which typically involve cooperation and compromise. I also ask them to search their
hearts and think about how much they may have
practiced these exercises vital to democracy. It is, of

[16] Benjamin Franklin's Final Speech in the
Constitutional Convention, from the notes of
James Madison, available online at http://www
.pbs.org/benfranklin/pop_finalspeech.html.

course, much easier to burrow with the like-minded than to engage meaningfully those who disagree, but such engagement is what democracy looks like.

Education, participation, practice in cooperation and compromise—all these efforts aim to build public trust in the working of our democratic institutions. In *The Plague,* Albert Camus helps us to understand why that trust, as well as why a rule of law, is so important. At the end of the book, the narrator explains why he has recounted the history of the plague that ravaged Oran, in what is perhaps an allegory of the Nazi occupation of France. Because, he says, he wants readers to know how the people of Oran reacted, for better or for worse, to that plague. Because he wants them to know what a doctor is—a person who, without discussion or theorizing, directly and simply brings help to those who need it. Above all, because the plague germ never dies. It goes into remission, lurking in the attics, the file cabinets, the closets, only to reemerge and again send its rats, for the learning or the misfortune of man, into a once-happy city.

THE AUTHORITY OF THE COURT

The rule of law is an important weapon, though not the only weapon, in our continuous fight against the plague germ.

I am an optimist. The rule of law has weathered many threats, but it remains sturdy. I hope and expect that the Court will retain its authority, an authority that my stories have shown was hard-won. But that authority, like the rule of law, depends on trust, a trust that the Court is guided by legal principle, not politics. Structural alteration of the Court motivated by the perception of political influence among justices can only feed that same perception, further eroding the public's trust. There are no shortcuts to trust. Trust in the Court, without which our system cannot function, requires knowledge, it requires understanding, it requires engagement—in a word, it requires work, work on the part of all citizens. And we must undertake that work together.

ACKNOWLEDGMENTS

I very much appreciate the thoughts, criticisms, and ideas that Paul Gewirtz has provided after reading and rereading early versions. I also appreciate the thoughts and guidance that Cass Sunstein, Martha Minow, and George and Lois de Menil have provided, as well as the work of my editors at Harvard University Press, George Andreou and Simon Waxman. I thank them, and many others as well.